Also by Norbert Hirschhorn

Poetry
A Cracked River Slow Dancer Poetry,
London 1999

Mourning in the Presence of a Corpse
Dar al-Jadeed, Beirut 2008

Monastery of the Moon Dar al-Jadeed,
Beirut 2012

*To Sing Away the Darkest Days—Poems
Re-imagined from Yiddish Folksongs* Holland
Park Press, London 2013

Stone. Bread. Salt. Holland Park Press,
London 2018

Once Upon a Time in Aleppo (a bilingual
Arabic-English co-translation with Fouad M.
Fouad) The Hippocrates Press, London 2020

Over the Edge Holland Park Press, London 2023

Memoir
*To Heal the World: My Life in Medicine,
Poetry, and Public Health* Sloan Publishing,
Cornwall-on-Hudson 2022

. . . endless forms most beautiful . . .

. . . endless forms most beautiful . . .

poems by norbert hirschhorn

La Rive Press

La Rive Press
Minneapolis, MN

Front cover art: Paul Sérusier, *Le Talisman*, 1888, Musée d'Orsay, Paris. Artwork in the public domain; image available from Wikimedia Commons.
Cover and book design by Molly Mortimer, Mayfly book design

ISBN: 979-8-218-76393-0

Library of Congress Catalog Number: 2025917438
First Printing: 2025

Carillon for Cynthia

Was it the ten yellow roses, or just my smile,
To evoke your crinkled laughter, making
Nothing else yet everything become worthwhile?

In my dreams I hear parades,
Peals of your laughter filling my head
As I tease and joke in murmured love bites.

In my dreams I hear parades —
Flotillas of birds, bells, streamers of light.
How I tease and joke in little love bites

When we hold each other nested like spoons
Among birds, bells, streamers of light.
Each night a rising full moon

As we hold each other nested like spoons,
Nothing else yet everything becomes worthwhile,
Neither rising nor setting full moon.

Was it roses or bells or—perhaps—your smile?

Contents

A Wretched Blue Sky

I feel ill when I see a perfect blue sky. *Blue skies, smilen' at me* ♪ ... may mean hurrah for some, but what about drought? No rain for months, birches & sycamores parched, crazy pavement of cracked earth. Or Sahara, or Sinai, where blue rules until a khamsin enrages sand & dust to pierce the day (cover your mouth & nose with a Tuareg scarf) until the next catastrophe: black risen clouds & raining debris—blue sky seen through an obliterated ceiling.

Abu Muhammed – God Preserve

(Lebanon, *ca.1930 - 2014*)

My right foot put up on the shoeshine caddy, his brush removes construction dust & dabs on creams with an ice-lolly stick, spreads by sponge, then *taps* under my toe... 85 or so, tiny, belt high on flat waist, white frond of hair, lit cigarette, on a low stool in the shade across from the AUB campus Main Gate where for decades he's polished shoes of presidents, profs & students (when they wore leather) ... *tap* for the left wingtip's turn, followed by wax spread & smoothed by his fingers ... *tap*, right wingtip waxed, then a two-handed brushing like squirrels chasing around & over to reveal the high gloss, & with a motley cloth... *snap!* his masterwork, done. I went out gladly into the sun.

AUB—American University of Beirut

2

Amok

The Junior Minister has just laughed politely at *Bapak*'s one-thousandth time retold joke. *Bapak* always tells small jokes on himself to make others feel at ease. He tries to get *Bapak*'s attention to an exceptionally urgent matter for the Ministerial Council. (Mouse-like titters from the others.) *Bapak* levels warm, brown eyes on him: the matter is being appropriately discussed at appropriate levels. Others shuffle papers, shift in chairs—they want to piss, smoke, check exchange rates. Now he pleads with his mates: consider the urgency, consider the consequences. (Sniggers this time, the matter is being considered by not being considered) The Junior Minister stiffens upright, his right arm begins to twitch uncontrollably, his face distorts in silent spasms, a small ooze of white spittle emerges like a worm from one corner of his mouth. Everyone looks away. *Bapak* examines the man coolly, not unkindly; then turns his gaze upward, to the ceiling, at the crack & peel of paint, how like the map of the great Indonesian archipelago they resemble: here, Irian Jaya; there, Aceh. The seizure stops. The meeting closes. The man is out sick for several days. When he returns, his desk is gone.

Bapak—an honorific for a distinguished Indonesian man

Back Into the Future

Have you ever been in a supermarket & seen someone who looked like your dead father? Spooky. Well, just yesterday, I almost called out to him, something I might have avoided when he was living. Anyway, we would've been speaking in different dialects, like now with my children, grandchildren. If the future is a foreign country, it's up to me to learn their language. Same deal with cities—built on ancient garbage they're all meters higher now. If I put my ear to the ground, I imagine whispers, laughter, sobbing, cries of orgasm that layers of soil, mud, rock, volcanic effusions haven't silenced. Those voices yearned for a future, achieved or not. Futures unachieved are only pruned or dead hopes—so when I try to remember my past, it's to revisit the branches of what could have been; mostly journeys of regret. Ah, regret, a negative mirror, showing my back, walking away. We don't go into the future; future comes into us. By the way, close up, he didn't look like my father at all.

Bad Start to a University Poetry Conference

4 am, the polyester sheets decide to slither off the plastic mat, the a/c kicks into low-drone, slow-speed dental drill mode, the kind favored by Nazi dentists, & I'm awake for good. Mind-wrestle a line of poetry, lose. Wait for first light, go to jog on 45 mph Main Street—bad judgment as a late night/early morning 75 mph pickup truck roars by & with no shoulder for retreat, I fall into the roadside foliage, scratched up by thorns, spines, prickles. He never saw me. Trembling, I thought it might have been winter before they found my decomposed body, picked apart by fishers & crows. The air foul with damp & fog, my hip sore, I nearly doze off shaving. His birthday today, my old friend's incandescent mind has powered down to 15 watts. Also today, I'm due to pay child support but the local post office doesn't sell money orders, orders me downtown where it's strictly cash—the ATM line three blocks long & hot besides, I turn to face the audience behind me ready to declaim on life being nasty, brutish, short; find myself face-to-face with my Muse, that dancer, who bestows her gorgeous wide-mouthed smile, & I shiver up to my ears.

Beggars of Beirut

1.

Something smashed his hips—a car bomb, a
building—leaving him jack-knifed, bent square, a
large brown dog, with flip-flops on his hands to
pad home with. He teeters in the roadway, one
hand offered to motorists passing. Sometimes a
thrown coin rolls into the gutter, a bill flutters off
in a breeze. Never mind, he'll retrieve them later.

2.

A   lumpish   woman,   huddled,   muttering,
someone's mother, put out each morning on a
camp chair, all weathers. On her lap, a 'poor box'
holding a handful of Chiclet packs no one dare
buy: just leave the money, no piastres either. Her
business is rage.

3.

Clubfoot, big smile, thorny moustache, crutches
since youth; he trawls the Corniche at sunup for
walkers, for joggers who know him by name:
Walid. Midday he works the falafel stand crowd &
at evening rush-hour on a roundabout median.
This is his job. He does it well.

4.

A waddly old woman, anyone's grandmother, dropped off each morning by the seaside, sits lengthwise on a backless bench; in her lap a shawl, an umbrella, an apron to catch charity. To each & every she cries, *May God bless you, your family! lengthen your life! give you well-being! bless your eyes!* She may levitate.

Chasing After Jesus, AD 5000

He'd heard rumors from a far galaxy, parsecs & parsecs away, of places where Jesus had returned—yet not to Earth, where we insist the mystery first arose. Or, would the Christ come to us only when all other corners of the cosmos were harrowed?

So, he set out for those remote places: *Why yes, Jesus was here, eons ago. If you find Him, tell how we wait.* He pressed on—*Yes, a few years ago... & on—Yes! A few months ago... Yes! Yesterday... Ah, you just missed Him...*

Without regret: in his pilgrimage for grace now at a close, with nothing more to lose nor gain, humbled, bereft, bare, he landed at last at the remotest place any could reach, to find *rainbows*: doubles, trebles, circles & crowns, the sky on fire.

Depression

From under the bathroom sink comes Soft Scrub
Cleanser, Heavy Duty Lysol, Spic & Span, Windex,
whisk-broom & scoop, a small white pail, an old
grey undershirt (stiff, curled) & I lift the toilet
seat, spray under the porcelain lip, move down
the sloping bowl, reach for the toilet brush, scrub
hard at brown specks, flush, restore the brush,
lower the seat; wet the undershirt, squirt Soft
Scrub to polish sink & tub, taps & spigots, rinsing
the cloth: squeeze, wipe, rinse, rinse again; spray
Windex on the medicine cabinet mirror, the
fumes running up my nose; stoop with broom &
scoop to sweep up hairs from the hard, white
tiles: hers long, silky, red; mine short, corkscrew,
grey; & make believe I'm a bent-backed Chinese
farmer planting rice: step, plant, step in the
sucking mud; or I'm a Yugoslav partisan picking
off Nazis: one behind the toilet, four behind the
door; fill the white pail with Lysol & water as hot
as my hand can stand, soak the *Stanley Kowalski*
undershirt, go down on my knees, now I'm a
pilgrim crawling to a sacred house in Bosnia,
visions of the Virgin; or I'm a night-shift slavey in
a high-rise office lavatory forever fluorescent, tile
by tile, rinse & squeeze, wet & wash—OMG,
more hairs wriggling like larvae; hopeless, I back

up to hearth & door, wipe my sweating face, slap
my cheek to kill a crawling hair & by mistake
knock off my glasses, fall backwards on my ass &
— who the fuck imagined it could come to this?
— begin to cry.

Diaspora,

dispersion, from *speirein*, to scatter or sow. We flourish like wildflowers, like weeds everywhere:

Jesus, Einstein, Marx & Freud, & don't forget Sandy Koufax who wouldn't pitch on Yom Kippur.

Chinese food better in Chinatown, pizza best in Little Italy; be sure to have a kasha knish at Yonah Schimmel's on Houston Street (pronounce it Howston).

Diaspora is good, keep it, nourish it, savor it, spread it, even when pesticides try to annihilate it: Roundup©, Zyklon B.

Directions

My ancestors came from Africa once, footprints preserved in Laetoli tuff, a family walking side-by-side, foraging for waterholes, fruit trees, safe haven.

I was in a rain forest once, tracking with our Wayana Indian guide under a canopy of monkey calls & insect buzz when with sheepish grin he announced: *We're lost.* We had to wait for another tribesman to come, show us the way.

I was in Deutschland once, my father sleeping rough, evading the Gestapo until we could all escape. My mother wore a crucifix, put me to breast, her blue-eyed blonde baby.

I was in a marriage once, no idea how to get somewhere I didn't know, searching for love where it couldn't be found.

Now in Minnesota, I often give directions to drivers, which, since I own no car, put them at mercy of one-way streets; they're far gone when I realize how wrong I was; wonder if they ever got to where they wanted to go.

Now I think about directions I've always needed: How to be good, which way to heaven.

Edgeland

It was, still is, known as the Green Line, a north-south civil war track a few meters wide, dividing East Beirut from West Beirut; Muslims in the latter, Christians in the former. Today, the line extends south to the airport separating Hezbollah Shia Muslims from Sunni Muslims. During the civil war, snipers fired east to west, west to east, day & night, picking off any unfortunate trying to cross, perhaps to get to a hospital, school, a certain shop, a job or family. Along the line were checkpoints with armed militiamen, whose sect memberships were not always certain. Show the wrong ID, wrong kind of name, & you'd be kidnapped for ransom, or killed on the spot. After the war the line became a demarcation zone, overgrown with wild green weeds, inhabited by rats & feral cats. Potholes filled with rancid water, ankle twisters if you dare now to walk the line. Buildings on either side stand pock-marked with bullet holes, windows bricked in once hiding the snipers. The fabulous Holiday Inn, thirty stories high, became a free-fire zone six months after its ceremonial opening. Decades later, the nation is broken as bankers, politicians & old warlords steal the people's money, assassins destroy a mother's dreams.

i.m. Lokman Slim

Ein Heldenleben

In the artless beginning, Edenic paintings —
flowering forest, lush undergrowth, hawks sailing
against the blue—& in the lower left-hand
corner, a signature, the artist's whimsy, a little
big-eared country mouse, nibbling petals. ¶ With
golden maturity—lightning to the east, trees
heavy with durian, a python draped like a
question mark, & now the rodent, sharper
toothed, not cute, has chewed its way through
bark & branch near the center of the scene. ¶ In
works of rage, the rat has consumed more than
half the pastorale, leaving volcanoes exploding,
rivers on fire, earthquake fissures. ¶ In an empty
studio—the beast has eaten the canvas, the
palette, the brush....

Encounter

At the local grocery store a shrunken old man,
straggled beard, Jewish surely, & his tiny wife (too
much lipstick) ponder over which pesto to try; it's
been tomato sauce up to now. I help them select
a good brand, if a bit pricey, & they thank me.

We talk about pasta sauces, chat about the
weather. Just then I have this interior vision:
They're holding hands, each carrying a small
suitcase, walking along a cobbled street, too slow
for the men with boots, guns, thumbs in their
belts, & I have to turn away before they see me
cry.

Fairy Tale in Six Voices:

The Prologue

Once upon a time, a young woman – beautiful, good, true – lived in a forest hut with her poor but honest parents. One day, a Prince came by on horseback & looking out for a bit of mischief, began to court her. Her parents, knowing what could come, tried to talk sense: *We're beneath his station, he'll break your heart, we need you here,* & so forth. But she was ecstatic; it had never happened before, probably would never again. You see, although she was lovely, virtuous, etc., she had a deformity, tuberculosis of the spine from childhood. But she was too happy to think clearly; & the Prince, perhaps a little in love, appeared not to notice. One day he rode up to the little hut saying, *Get yourself ready, I want to introduce you to the King and Queen.* Her parents, wanting only her happiness, sold their cow, pawned their dishes, mortgaged their little plot so she could wear something decorous, lovely for the meeting. *But only one thing,* said the Prince. *Yes, darling, anything,* she replied. *When we enter the Royal Court, try to stand up straight.*

The Voices

The Young Woman's Parents (a duet): We were idiots to think this could even be. All that time we deliberately stayed in the forest, away from people, so our daughter would never have cause to be unhappy.

The King: Reginald disappoints. A gadabout, he has never buckled down to study statecraft and the arts of war. So, when he announced he had been taken in by this opportunist with her mincing gait, I was ready to disinherit the fool, send him out of the Kingdom.

The Queen: He is a good son. Headstrong like his father, but a romantic like me. Perhaps it was something about the zephyrs, the honeysuckle, forest trails surprising at each turn. When the King courted me, I too was cloistered, shy, worshipful. I would have liked to have met this young innocent.

The Prince: So imagine how I felt! Well, she was sweet. I thought she was just being humble, not a hunchback. Christ, I'd never hear the end of it from my mates, never mind all the goosey gossip. I had some gold coins sent over.

The Young Woman: It was a dream, and so it sweetened my life. I know no one lives happily ever after, especially not in a castle. But if the King had condemned him to exile, I would have gone with him. My parents and I are moving deeper into the forest.

Filial Piety

Gale force squalls blustered the Heath, darkening down Parliament Hill, chasing patches of blue & one sad whisp of rainbow. Air now calm, now roiled, what next to expect?

Somehow, it made me think of the pupil who came to Confucius to ask permission to mourn his father for six months instead of the customary twelve. The sage replied with the Mandarin equivalent of *do what you need to do.* After the youth had gone, Confucius, his face drawn in sorrow, turned to a second disciple: *How can we expect society to be virtuous if just anyone can fix the time of grief for a father?*

The storm blew in the windows of the old age home on the hill, bringing air & rain to the shut-aways, & smells of myrtle & grass. Those who could, escaped to wade the pond with swans, coots, herons.

Four Disciples

Master Wu Shei sent out four disciples, those readiest to benefit the world. He called Pupil Wei Min to his side to learn how each was spending his days. The first, Wei Min reported, teaches to hundreds across the country-side: Humility, compassion, evanescence, mutability. *Wonderful*, replied the Master, *to show the road is to gain the road*. The second acolyte incises runes on bone, blocks of wood, to be inked, printed on rice paper & wind banners. *Excellent. He spreads prayers like clouds, like moonlight.* The third has retired to a grotto where he fasts & meditates, meditates & fasts. *Ah, a body in purification gives succor to us all. And of my favorite disciple, what news?* Pupil Wei Min covered his face. 'He reflects on the suffering in the world, does nothing but weep.' Master Wu Shei rocked slowly. *If I praised him, he would not be pleased.* He rose, bent over & raked the stones.

Fragments From the East

From the top corner window of the Cecil Hotel, where once we made love, I look out on the harbor as blue as Cleopatra's lapis lazuli, the air blushing with the coming of spring & pubescent boys polish shiny the brass breasts of Mother Egypt seated beneath the statue of Saad Zaghloul. ⸲ Linen curtains shield the portholes distilling breezes through their fringes: relief for the fevered sleepers below. Something strokes me within this vessel, if breath, if hand, tilling me towards the Promised Land. ⸲ I pick up pennies from the street, I'm always looking down. Not pennies falling from heaven but drifters from under the earth where dead saints lie, pennies on their eyes, calling me down. ⸲ My window slips open inside each night as jasmine breezes coil wounds on my body. Black crowned night herons shadow the Ottoman moon & a far-away flute weeps its threnody. ⸲ I have little left save my wounds—dearest thief come now to embezzle my heart.

Ghost Stories

We sat around the fireplace one Halloween trying
to see if we could still scare ourselves silly. My
neighbor in the Victorian said its builder was a
retired whaler with a stump for a leg & on windy
nights he has heard thump, thump on the back
stairs. Another told how she once felt a tearing, a
ripping, across her belly, like when you peel an
infected scab away from flesh, that screeching
pain; later, the phone rang, her son, stabbed in a
park—but alive! thank God. My turn came
around & I said how dull I felt. I had nothing of the
sort to tell, but I lied.... Two days after my mother
died, I saw her shadow, her perfect silhouette, at
the foot of my bed. My voice came out too small,
too high—'Ma? Ma?'—& it said nothing,
nothing. It just stood there, hating me.

Haibun for My American Despair

When life & television were benign, all problems solved in 54 minutes, I'd get tucked into bed, knowing I was safe in the hands of whatever loving god still existed, in the land of the free, the home of pure water, good air. I'm eighty-seven now, a survivor, actuarily about three more to go, half of those in one state of decay or another.

> late April storm
> cherry blossoms torn
> scattered
>
> empty wheelchair

As I approach the penultimate page of my own book of life, I see earth heating up unnaturally; prime forests burning; animals erased; pandemics finding our too large population good to eat; children dying at sea & in the streets; fascists reelected. I'm like the boy who stubs his toe in the dark: too old to cry, too hurt to laugh.

He Sweeps the Kitchen Floor,

with bristles of broom plucked from the brilliant
yellow flowers cascading down three hills that
enfold the monastery, each whisker picking
debris from cracks between the tiles with a
soughing like noise made by his Master after a
bowl of congee, removing runaway sesame
seeds, desiccated insects, cook's errant black
hairs, but leaving rice grains behind the door to
feed the young mouse (he thinks: of eight grades
of charity the highest to provide honest work),
strokes the debris into piles, one per quadrant of
floor, stoops like a woman poking seedling rice
one-by-one into black sucking mud, sweeps them
to the dustpan, leaving finer lines to be re-
gathered, re-swept (he thinks: if he could shrink
in size along with each thinner line of dust, would
there not always be dust?), & laves the tiles on
hands & knees with a modestly wetted
moonwort cloth, rinsing & wringing into the
bamboo bucket, its soapy water growing darker
with each rinse like winter evenings (he studies
each tile: here the piece that resembles his birth-
house whose sodded roof inclined to the ground
& fed Father's four pigs), & his knees begin to
ache their familiar ache: One snowy winter, he'd
returned to his village & found all things silent, a
charred corpse leaning out the window of his
house like Mother calling down, a single chicken
picking among two black, bodiless heads resting

on pillows of ash. He had just learned from his Master how to be still, fell to his knees & crawled through cinders & trash, past the still-smoking timbers of market stalls (not even a cabbage remained), kneed his way along the icy pebbled road, each facet of stone slicing his skin, kneed out of the village, over the three hills, & into the glade of his now only home (& now rises slowly, now ponders the glow of the kitchen floor, now prepares for morning meditation).

How Many Chances
(*A fictional memoir*)

Those were his happiest days, yet the most despairing. It was almost love at first sight, surely by the second time they met: with her blue eyes, red hair, a concert pianist, a world-sophisticate — which he wasn't—& the way she walked. He swore he'd never take her for granted, he promised he'd never intrude on her space or time, thinking of course about his own diminished state. He was a clumsy lover at first, needy really, but it amused her, he was so honest, without the façade she found in other men who, at core, feared her. She was patient with him because she saw a twinkle, some beginning lightness, like a person emerging from years in a dungeon into the light, & she was an artist of light, renewal. She taught him how to pleasure her, to take pleasure to himself, which felt to him strange: exhilarating, yet frightening. How many chances does a person need, or get, to set life right?

In the end,
he couldn't choose, couldn't dare. *I,* he once smiled sadly, *I am unhappily married, while you, sweetheart, are happily unmarried.* So, when she returned from yet another tour, on a Thursday, light rain, cold wind, & he had greeted her once again with yet another cluster of yellow roses, she told him quietly, firmly that she had taken a lover,

one with no impediment, a bit cruel perhaps, but
without illusions of love. This satisfied her.

                       Small deaths:
over the passing time he thought he saw her —
that strideful walk—threading the crowd in
Times Square, turning a corner off Piccadilly,
across a piazza in Rome, & he'd wave, chase after.
But it was always a shape-shifter, a Morgan le
Fay, someone else he might yet catch up to, ask
to coffee, dinner, bed; each time it made him feel
like a man drowning, drowning, not waving.

Last line an adaptation of Stevie Smith's *Not Waving but
Drowning*

I was the world in which I walked...*

Greyhound terminal   last bus to Duluth
homeless man on wood bench under a thin
blanket   lone barista locks up shop   pocket park
with hooded figures leaning against trash bins
bulbs   out   blinking   neon   sign   advertising
Gold   Meda   Flou   full   moon   scowls   like
King Kong above a high-rise late night jogger
fox   crossing   road   disappears   into   shadowy
hedge   café chairs stacked on tables   food
vendor sleeping beneath his four-wheeled cart
Gate 5   Duluth   All Aboard   Now

*Wallace Stevens, *Tea at the Palaz of Hoon*

In the Beginning

was a certain bird, & the bird had an inaudible chirp, & God saw it was good. But the bird pleaded for identity, a sound other birds would hear, then respect. All songs had been given out, none left, but God took pity on this one last, tiny thing, & made its wings beat so fast they hummed.

Lamentation

In Union Square, Lubavitchers lit up a giant wooden nine-armed Hanukkah candelabrum — 150-watt bulbs, not candles. Even with his back turned he knows I am Jewish & he will whirl about to ask, *Are you Jewish?* & if I say yes, he will haul me into the *Mitsvahmobile* to make me put on phylacteries, which I've not done since my bar mitsvah, & also promise to divorce my *shiksa* wife standing alongside. Meanwhile, kitty-corner across the Square, in the creche ("paid for by private funds"), the Holy Family waits, lovingly refusing to reconvert. So, for the first time in my life I said, No. Again, he asked me, *Are you Jewish,* & once again he asked me, *Are you Jewish?* Three times I denied.

Last Words

My 'birth,' if one can call it such, waking from a formless, soundless void into the bright fluorescence of a nursing home—hospital cot, fed by pap. I'm still amused recalling those elder years: forgetful, querulous, obsessing on all my failures, but as I grew down into mid-life wisdom, sliding through years of scrabbling for success, I became generous with colleagues, helpful to all, envying none. Wisdom, yes, from the heady experience of living. What I now knew of life & loss I taught my children; none of whom broke my heart. My wife & I went from hand-holding love to glorious lust unsullied by affairs or rancor even as we slipped past each other along our two-headed arrow of time. I was most gladdened by my vigorous youth—no drugs, no drink, nor rebellion. School mates looked up to me as their leader. They called me a child prodigy, yet I wore my learning lightly. It was then I first confronted the ultimate conundrum: How did this... this *Entity* become Me? I sensed the answer would come only when after an infancy of blesséd suckling I returned to her veiled womb, floating to the sounds of *lup dup lup dup*, a rhythm of *Release*, blended into *Self,* whose last words I heard were: *yes, yes.*

Inspired by F. Scott Fitzgerald's, *The Curious Case of Benjamin Button.*

Mahmoud Darwish & Charles Darwin in Conversation

(a cento)

MD:

The reader will wonder what poetry says to us in time of disaster... On this earth there is that which deserves life.

CD:

Certainly, no fact in the long history of the world is so startling as the wide and repeated exterminations of its inhabitants.

MD:

Against barbarity, poetry can resist only by confirming its attachment to human fragility like a blade of grass growing on a wall while armies march by.

CD:

If I had my life to live over again, I would have made a rule to read some poetry and listen to some music at least once every week.... The loss of these tastes is a loss of happiness.

MD:

If a writer were to compose a successful piece/ describing an almond blossom, the fog would rise/ from hills the hills, and people, all the people, would say:/ This is it! / These are the words of our national anthem.

CD:

It is not the strongest of the species that survives, not the most intelligent that survives. It is the one that is the most adaptable to change.

MD:

I defend the need of poets for a tomorrow and for memories at the same time; I defend the tree that birds clothe, as a country and a place of exile; I defend a moon that is still suitable for a love poem; I defend an idea shattered by the frailty of its holders, and I defend a country hijacked by legends.

CD:

There is grandeur in this view of life, with its several powers, having been originally breathed into a few forms or into one; and that, whilst this planet has gone cycling on according to the fixed law of gravity, from so simple a beginning endless forms most beautiful and most wonderful have been, and are being, evolved.

Motel from Hell

      the kind where you wedge the back of a chair under the door knob & check beneath the bed before going to sleep

      where the proprietor cleans his fingernails with a hunting knife & you wake from a nightmare, sliding off polyester sheets

      where every pickup truck has a gun rack, my accent & clothes giving me away as some wuss from 'back east'

      where 'free breakfast' means weak coffee, Fruit Loops, jelly donuts, a waitress chewing gum ducking out to smoke an unfiltered Lucky Strike

      in my rear-view mirror, a neon sign flashes —

VACANCY VACANCY VACANCY

Mourning Dove Comes to Call

Oh good! His awning window is open this
morning, enough to scatter biscuit bits on the sill.
My favorite: Walker's Pure Butter Shortbread.

I've been watching him

when I think he's not watching me. Grey, old, in a
room with single bed, desk, lounge chair,
television (on all the time, sound off). A
telephone. The only visitors I can see: a woman
to bathe him, another to give meds, a third to
deliver food on a tray.

He dresses himself:

trousers, shirt (food stains), unzipped cardigan.
He writes on a yellow pad, shuffles papers on the
desk crowded with framed photographs; a stack
of newspapers. Diplomas hang on the wall, that
painting of an old man saying grace over a loaf of
bread.

Oh. No biscuit bits today.
Or yesterday.

My Father No Longer Exists

His was the body I saw in coma. His the body I saw in a mortician's parlor laid in a pine coffin, dressed in a white tunic, made up to disguise the ravages of a life: rouge, reddened lips, slicked hair — & cold to my touch. His the body viewed one last time before lowered into the ground followed by dirt, rocks, & prayers into perpetual darkness. Were I a nineteenth-century grave robber looking to sell corpses to anatomists, I might have seen him there one last time. Not unlikely—In medical school I dissected a formaldehyded man in his thirties—gaunt, anonymous (I named him "Chuckie")—stripping away skin, nerve, muscle, down to bone; nearly nothing now, like the turkey carcass left over after Thanksgiving.

Ode to My Body

Oh body, my body, my buddy since birth, with me through thick & thin, fair & foul, I gave you pleasure, you gave me same—remember when we nearly—well, wasn't that something & here we've been together for decades, now approaching the shades—oh buddy, please, don't quit on me now.

Ode to the Cicadas

(Brood X, 2021)

A sound like castanets thrumming in synchrony, super-bugs by the billions, creating a cacophony that once drowned out Bob Dylan's singing (yes, that happened). The 17-year *Brood Ten* has now emerged from underground to molt, eat, mate, die. Their progeny will return to ground, maturate, return just when I turn one-hundred (deaf, blind).

Along with their sexy fire engine red eyes, males clack their tymbals to court females like sex-starved Neapolitan tenors. Their carcasses litter the roadways & forest floor — dozens per square foot—fertilizing trees, make nibbles for birds, squirrels, snakes, & even some people. Cars crush them to a slippery, skiddy pulp.

When all humans die off from some sudden pandemic cicadas won't care (nor rats, nor roaches), they'll just keep on singing.

Old Man at Assisi

Here on Monte Subasio above the stone village
he looks on as *giovani* flirt & kiss beside the grotto
where the saint kept vows of poverty & chastity.
The old man has to laugh—by those rules he too
is Franciscan, though hardly by choice. Would he
could reclaim those headlong days, to be like
those angels on the mountain, guiding parasails
for lift & eddy, reluctant to return to ground. But
what appears in his mirror is a wild poppy pressed
inside a book: wrinkled, smell of feral fields.

Prayer in Spite of Myself

Pig-eater, *shiksa*-wedder, God-denier, Arab-lover. Dispossessed, displaced, disinherited, disillusioned, stranded on a melting floe of assimilation.

Loving Judaism too much & not enough. Zionism: baked so deep into the brain—would be like plucking out blueberries from a muffin. Doctor, go for it, make me *Un*-Zionist.

Jesus, Einstein, Marx & Freud: That's what Jews do.

Renewal Soup

Since all of life is just a way of going home, I'm here again, in love with you, my dearest, taking the *passeggiata,* evening stroll, in the piazza. I wear my broad straw hat with the paisley band, & greet the stylish citizens of Siena, "Buona sera, buona sera."

I first came here in '38 brought by my parents. The happiest time of their lives, they said years later — giddy with relief at their escape, still certain they could get their parents out next. Who could blame them for succumbing to the warm Tuscan autumn, purple grapes, blood oranges, the large-hearted language & mellifluous people? The rhapsody ended when they heard the news—their parents had been murdered. (...*They didn't know how to run...they tied their wrists to the back of a truck and made them run...")* From then until their own deaths, they knew they had stolen the apple.

Millions of poppies in the fields across the farm where we stay, pointillist red on green. At night, a sparkle of fireflies. I feel weepy, afraid, for if I say this (is) (was) the happiest time of my life (it is!) (it was!), I've dared be happier than my parents, deciding to survive even when others might drown. In *The Universal Judgment*—an altar panel in the Basilica—the saved, to the left, draped in damask coats & moiré gowns, walk about in orchards of figs, arbors of grapes, amazed at their escape; they gather in clusters in quiet recollection with family & old friends, amazed, forever amazed. To the right are the damned: naked, draped by monstrous hominids mutilating breasts & genitals; bodies piled in fiery baths & frigid pools, rapes, poisonous vapors.

The dark between the final chitter of the swifts & the aubade of the thrush is called *le ore blu*, the Blue Hours, when the land relaxes, blue vapors float through the trees, the trees breathe in the heat, & stars drift in eternal promenade—while in the cemeteries of Siena, lovers drift in dreamless, permanent sleep. Old stone houses lean toward each other as if in quiet recollection, woven together by cobblestone lanes. Each way seems to return upon itself, familiar but different — with just a small tilt of the head, an infinity of compositions: chimney on bell, bell on basilica, angels on clotheslines, a geranium pot red-spotting a sill, angles & corners & curves. By chance we look up to see a blood-orange moon rising in the needle's-eye between two steeples.

Each way comes back to way. It was on this same cobbled lane I once told you I couldn't decide. What if you had then turned to the left & I to the right? I believe our ways would have returned, returning each to Siena, our bolt-hole from life.

Wouldn't your henna-red hair catch my eye, disappearing down a curved lane, or across a piazza with Mass just letting out?

A Gregorian chant resonates, coheres to millennial layers of hum impressed on the permanent stone. Saint Catherine of Siena went to a man about to be hanged & *brought him to a state of grace,* refreshed him, consoled & forgave his years of rage as orphan, cut-purse, bravo, gave him faith of an existence beyond himself—how I feel when, in my moments of incendiary self-loathing, you call, & your voice, like baptism, cooling me. If grace is true, the mussels in garlic & cool Vernaccia, a hot bath with you, that moment we both chewed your hair slipped into your mouth, are gifts beyond understanding.

St. Bernadino's skull lies in a glass & gold reliquary, along with long bones, knuckles of vertebrae, scarp of pelvis. He was canonized for reviving freshly dead children. I've done that myself & more than once. The real miracle was the opportunity. Who & what gave me to my life? Had my father that night turned to the left, my mother to her right, surely wouldn't another night have still brought me to writing this, have brought me? Perhaps I **am** that other night.

Ribollita
is a Tuscan soup made of white beans, a head of purple garlic, knuckles of old bread, kale, white cabbage, vegetables & stock. It's meant to be reheated & stored, reheated & stored, for unexpected guests who come to the door. The soup is renewed by adding in more old bread, more stock, more beans.

In a chapel of the Duomo of Siena a young woman in bronze, life-size, holds up a salver filled with oil — the candle lit daily—in adoration of the Madonna & Child in the niche. As clouds play across the sky, light from the oriel window strokes her beatific face & long-braided hair. I circle her & circle her; I almost want to take her in my arms until, with no embarrassment, stroke her permanent cheek. I feel something like a moment of grace. I will die, but not for what I am.

Bless stones. Bless children, Bless light. Bless swifts. Bless saints. Bless soup.

Song for Cynthia

At Union Square Farmers Market—Kombucha to
Bombay Brunch, bomba rice to basmati—two
black men are noodling out some jazz—alto
clarinet & acoustic blues guitar—their sweet
notes flittering in the cool twilit air like the
cabbage white butterflies dancing between trees.
I plunked down my dollar, price of admission, &
man with the reed whispered to man with the
pick, amounting to, I think, *Play something silky
for this old white guy.*

They riffed on How Deep is the
Ocean:

*And if I ever lost you, how much
would I cry?*

The Blessèd Mother

They used my mother as slavey: **Come here! Carry this! Bring that!** shouting, because she spoke little English. She heard horses snuffling in their stalls. Spitfires overhead. At noon, her lunch half-hour, she heard church bells. 'The Angelus', said the Irish maids. 'Turn your thoughts to God and the Blessèd Mother.' In the garden, she sat under the laburnum tree, its golden chains reminding her of lindens in Vienna whose perfume infiltrated that last summer before their escape. Her toddler son was made to be still. He was still; & years after, still. A sepia photograph shows his lips trembling. She dries sweet red peppers for paprika to add to the goulash.

The Dough Not Taken

Two banks stood in a neighborhood, & sorry I couldn't heist from both & be one robber, long I stood & stared down the road as far as I could so not to get caught through any sloth.

Thus, I aimed at one within the square seeming to have more loot to its name with marble columns showing less wear, though as for the custom going there, people entered both just about the same.

But both that morning had cops stand out front, with guns and batons that thwack. So, I kept them for another day! Yet knowing how way leads on to way I doubted I should ever come back.

I shall be telling this with a sigh somewhere decades & decades hence: Two big banks stood in a square, & I—I held up neither, which, by the by, averted any consequence.

The Princess Who Thought She Was a Turkey

(Tale adapted from Rabbi Nachman of Bratzlav)

Once upon a time there was a Princess who thought she was a turkey. She refused to get dressed, walked with a waddle, spoke with a gobble. She hid beneath the galley table, pecking at fallen food. The King, desperate, promised the hand of his daughter to any man in the realm who could heal her. Many tried (charms, chains, potions, spells), none succeeded. One day, a *doula* came into town; one used to a hard scrabble life & sorrow, but also joy. She saw the broadside in the market & thought she could, at least, offer comfort. The King's viziers laughed, slapped their knees, but the Queen said, *Let her try, we have nothing to lose.* Rather than interrogating the Princess about her childhood, or shouting at her to stop being silly, the doula simply undressed, crawled beneath the table, & began to peck at the crumbs. After some days, the Princess asked the doula, *Who are you?* To which she replied, *I am a turkey.* The Princess, surprised, replied that she, too, was a turkey. They continued to forage together. After some weeks, the doula told the Princess, *You know, we can still be turkeys but turkeys who wear clothing,* & she put on a shift. The Princess, laughing, agreed to a chemise, then slippers, eventually her gown. She returned to the dining hall of the Palace, but whenever she wanted, she could still be a turkey, just like before. The doula went on her ways, just like before.

The Train

The Radegast train depot stood just outside the ghetto of Lodz. It was once used, in that unlovely German word, as an *Umschlagplatz*, meaning 'transshipment place.' My grandparents & dozens of other Jews were collected, packed into the nearly-cliché-named *cattle cars,* to be transported to the annihilation camp of Chelmno, thirty-eight kilometers away. Four years ago, I stood in the memorial plaza of the depot. Parked on the rails alongside the wood-frame waiting room were four original wagons, headed by a huge, black locomotive. A group of us climbed into one of the cars. It was night, dark, with only a few weak points of light trickling from smart phones. I suddenly felt wobbly, as if the train was beginning to move. I told this afterwards to my sweet young son who said, "I'm so sorry for what happened to you. Why is the world so cruel? I know I can be a little mean, but not like this, deep down inside I'm not like this."

For Robert

There Was Once a Certain Place

where a Potentate of the Old Way ordered murals to be painted on opposite walls of the Great Court by the most skilful artists of the Dominion, those from the West versus ones from the East. The motif assigned—*The Sublime*.

A thick tapestry divided the teams who for months laboured, eating, sleeping in place until the time for judgment. Up first, the Western artists' revelation: Edenic bliss as they imagined: cypresses, high grasses, orchards, nightingales, a river winding to the purple horizon. Then came the command, *Raise the curtain* revealing the Eastern team's work: a giant mirror, buffed to flawless precision. Here, the same Edenic bliss perfectly reflected: cypresses, high grasses, orchards, nightingales, a river winding to the purple horizon. Except, in the lower right corner, a young couple, hand-in-hand, walking away.

Based on a fable by Maulana Jalaladdin Rumi in *Mathnawi*

Things I Didn't Know I Loved

(after Nazim Hikmet)

finger-nail moon at sunset announcing my new
month   white fluff of cottonwood trees in spring
dress   smell of first rain off warm pavements I
didn't know I loved

I didn't know I loved squirrels chasing across the
high wire or the moon ghostly balloon floating
in the pre-dawn sky with beads of car lights
crossing the river

autumn leaves swirling in windy circles like
dervishes   or a willow tree—girl throwing hair
over her eyes I never knew I loved

I didn't know I loved that eagle pair rowing
through air or the great white cutter sailing over
the Mississippi—albino red-tailed hawk   avatar
come to bless

hummingbird   hovering   over   petunias
geraniums' rebirth after old heads lopped   what
pluck   missing her even when she's in the next
room things I didn't know I loved

Times There Are

when I shouldn't ever be driving at night. One time we were headed from Minneapolis to Sioux City, due southwest, a four-and-a-half-hour drive. It was for my wife's 25th high school reunion, to which she wanted to go only to see how her classmates had weathered the quarter century. The women, coiffed, in pumps & cocktail dresses, out for a good time. The men, bellied & balding, huddled to themselves, drinking shots & beer chasers. Most had never left Iowa. But I'm getting ahead of myself—that was the next evening. As these things go, we got a late start & found ourselves watching the sun set ahead of us faster than we could drive. Soon the six-lane highway turned to four, then two & it was dark. Coming straight on in the opposite lane were semis, behemoths, probably carrying hogs for slaughter by Mexicans or Somalis in the death houses of Minnesota, their headlights blinding as if daring me to drive head-on. When we reached our motel, I could barely uncurl my fingers to sign the register.

Twenty-Third Psalm for the Twenty-First Century

1. The carrion bird is my jailer; He leaves me bereft.

2. He maketh me lie down on bombed concrete, drink foul water.

3. He destroyeth my family, erases our name for His sadist's sake.

4. Yea, as I lie in the shadow of impending death, His despotic eye trembleth me, His beak & claws lacerate my flesh.

5. To the derision of my enemies, He tippeth my head into oblivion. His hatred runneth over.

6. Surely evil & cruelty will follow to the end of my days, & buried in this charnel house forever.

Two Tales From the Hasidim

I.

A Rebbe & his young disciple were on pilgrimage to a revered Tsaddik's tomb when they came upon a stream in spate. Near them was a young woman in long dress & head scarf – distressed, afraid to chance the crossing. The Rebbe lifted her gently onto his back, strode into the stream up to his waist, & crossed, the disciple following. Once on the other side, the men walked silently for a long while until the disciple said, *Master, pardon me, but you shouldn't have touched that woman.* The Rebbe thought a moment, & replied, *I put her down some time ago. Why are you still carrying her?*

II.

They tell this story of the Baal Shem Tov: Some calamity was facing the Jews. So he went into the forest, lit a special fire, said a special prayer, the disaster was averted. Decades later, another catastrophe was on the way, but his disciples had forgotten how to make that fire. Yet, the prayer still worked. Generations later, people forgot the words to that prayer, but still remembered this story, which sufficed. But now, after all that has happened to us, why do we keep retelling the story?

Adaptations from Martin Buber's Tales of the Hasidim.

Baal Shem Tov, 'Master of the Good Name' (ca.1700-1760), familiar form of Rabbi Israel ben Eliezer, founder of Hasidism.

Until the End of Time
(For Brian Greene)

Death I understand: my flesh rejoins the universe
like sea water escaping a cracked amphora. The
way, they say, I inhale molecules breathed out by
Jesus. Another kind of resurrection.

But how did I get here in the first place?

A little wanderer, in what green room was I
waiting to come on stage? In what bardo
antechamber awaiting summons, like a quantum
particle kept in suspense (there) (not there)? Or,
washing ashore from fathomless depths, laughing
& crying with my first breath.

& where did these luscious figs come from?

Variations on the Hand

His were large, fleshy, warm. Whenever he took mine, I felt comforted, safe. Lost in an air raid shelter once, in the dark, I felt about for his hand. After passing through some legs, some coats, became enveloped by his. I knew it.

Hers were small, bony, chilled. A sparrow fallen from a tree I feared to crush, but brought to my lips. Knuckles raised, swollen. I massaged them, gently. *Why are you so sad?   I don't know. I don't know.*

He & I greet one another in the manner of The Resistance: Right arms swinging in an arc from the level of the head, each palm slapping into the other's with the gusto sound of solidarity.

"Give a hand up, not a hand out." What am I to do seeing disheveled men sitting on cardboard holding signs written on by black magic marker: *hungry, homeless, need money for a bed tonight.* I shelter my eyes.

Left hand wears a wedding ring. Right hand with thumb on the detonator.

Vermont Farm Year in 1890

They survived the twelve-foot snow, now sit
frozen in the photograph, silver granules
freckling white solemn faces & calico. They
planned for their losses—pressing seven seeds
into each hole, rhyming,

One for the blackbird,
one for the crow,
one for the cutworm
four to let grow.

They planned for their losses, even children,

One for the measles,
one for the cold,
one for the bloody flux,
four to grow old.

Their names kept them upright: Asa, Ethan,
Abigail, Dwight, Hannah, Sarah, Nathaniel, Giles.
Their farms sprouted nouns & verbs, all blunt &
stubbled: hoe scythe bellows sieve flail
coulter felloe peavy yep nope mebbe

Work was played out in cadence: broadcast oat
seed, rye seed, buckwheat & barley; walk &
swing, a lot like dancing.

Rout out tussocks, haul out boulders, load up the stone-boat to build strong walls.

As you tread between the tombs (weeping angels & seraphim) please observe how oft there's two of her to one of him.

clean glean chop milk comb
card spin weed feed grind
cook bake curd churn pluck
sew treat teach birth suckle
        bury pray

They depleted the land of woods. Used themselves up, wore themselves out, made themselves do or did without.

Their epitaphs are everywhere—tumbleweed, dandelion seed, brambles shrouding cellar holes, stone walls tumbling down the fall line.

Based on an exhibit at Billings Farm & Museum, Woodstock, Vermont.

Visitation

At each beginning of each new beginning – school, job, retreat by the sea – he fell in love. Always the same person: solemn, thin, no makeup, a way of brushing back a strand that made him nearly cry with longing.

They'd walk along a corniche, fingers interlaced, or through woods, or through galleries, something about her hand he knew even in the dark.

Then—Gone. Gone.

He looked for her. Perhaps he saw her, or thought he saw her, threading the crowd off Piccadilly, across a square in Siena. He'd wave, or maybe tried to wave, call out her name but her name choked in his throat.

Much later, he woke to find her standing at the foot of his bed.

> *Who are you?* he whispered.
> *How did I ever come to know you?*

Wisconsin Death Trip

(for Warren Woessner)

Don't ask me why but in all small towns from Madison to La Crescent Minnesota (Route 14), cafés are closed up on Wednesdays & so we were happy to pull into the gravel parking lot of Ray J's American Grille, neon sign 'OPEN', parked our Honda CRV alongside a pickup truck, gun rack & all. The men inside sat on bar stools, heads down, murmuring, scalps covered with monogrammed baseball caps declaring allegiance to the Packers or feed stores or VFW, the walls lined with hunting posters & arcade game machines.

I got us coffee, half & half from plastic containers, & ordered cheese sandwiches (*cheese*, sure) on brown whole wheat bread. The tired proprietor said, *White bread, that's what we got around here.* Me, in my beret, didn't ask for brown sugar.

Wooden Door

Buildings lay in heaps of crushed stone against a cool blue sky. The camera rushes over the debris toward a cacophony of voices. A cluster of men emerges near a building that was standing moments before Israeli air strikes crushed it. They are carrying on a wooden door a girl, perhaps nine or ten, covered in dust—her hair, her pants, her little legs. It is urgent, the way this pack of men carries this girl, yelling at everyone in their way to move. She's silent at first, but then taking stock of how she's being transported by these men, the girl asks, matter-of-factly, "رايحة على المقبرة؟"—"Are we going to the cemetery?" It's chaos around them, but somehow, one of the men bending over this makeshift stretcher hears her question & immediately assures her, fiercely, loudly, "لا يا عمي هيك عايشة هيك مشاء الله عليكي زي القمر!"—"No, love, here you are, you're alive, your face beautiful like the moon!"

Excerpted from Pacinthe Mattar, journalist.
https://thewalrus.ca/in-gaza-language-is-all-we-have-left/

Acknowledgments

Directions *South Bank Poetry*

Fairytale in Six Voices *The Bluebird Word*

He Sweeps the Kitchen Floor *The Eleventh Muse*

Motel from Hell *La Presa*

Ode To My Body; Haibun for My American Despair; Visitation; Chasing After Jesus AD 5000; The Dough Not Taken; *Twenty-Third Psalm for the Twenty-First Century London Grip*

Old Man at Assisi *Phenotype*

Renewal Soup *A Cracked River* Slow Dancer Press

The Princess Who Thought She Was a Turkey *Iconoclast*

The Train *The Ravens Perch*

Variations on the Hand; Four Disciples; Back Into the Future; *I was the world in which I walked... The Mackinaw: a journal of prose poetry*

Vermont Farm Year in 1890 *The Ekphrastic Review*

Wisconsin Death Trip is the title of a
1973 historical nonfiction book by Michael
Lesy charting numerous sordid, tragic, &
bizarre incidents that took place in & around
Jackson County, Wisconsin between 1885 &
1900, primarily in the town of Black River Falls.
Caesura 2025 "Lit"

With gratitude to my poet friends, Jacqueline
Saphra, Marilyn Hacker, Marge Barrett, & my
wife Cynthia Myntti for close readings of the
manuscript in draft. Many thanks to the La Rive
Creative Writing Group in Minneapolis for
patient attention to a number of the poems, as
well as to my London Torriano Meeting House
poetry mates.

Thanks also to Robyn Roslak for tracking down
the correct citation for the cover art.

With gratitude to the Mayfly book design team—
Molly Mortimer, Ryan Scheife, Julie Scheife.

About the Author

Norbert Hirschhorn is a physician specializing in
international public health, commended in 1993
by President Bill Clinton as an "American Health
Hero." His poems have been published in over
three dozen journals & seven full collections in
the US, UK & Lebanon. See his poetry website,
bertzpoet.com & a summary of his career at
Wikipedia.